Wakpá Wanáği
Ghost River

Trevino L. Brings Plenty

The Backwaters Press

I would like to thank all my friends and family.
And a special thanks to my wife, Jade, for her loving support.

Also by Trevino L. Brings Plenty

Real Indian Junk Jewelry, The Backwaters Press, 2012

Book design by SR Desktop Services
Cover design by Bristol Creative, www.bristolcreative.com
Photo of the poet by Amy McMullen, copyright © 2015, used by permission.

First Printing: April 2015

Published by: The Backwaters Press
James Cihlar, Editor
Greg Kosmicki, Editor Emeritus
3502 N. 52nd Street
Omaha, Nebraska 68104-3506
thebackwaterspress@gmail.com
http://www.thebackwaterspress.org

ISBN 13: 978-1-935218-37-1

Library of Congress Control Number: 2015933065

Acknowledgments

I would like to thank these journals, which housed some of my work: *As/Us Journal*, *Denizen Gallery*, *Portland Art Museum*, *Red Ink Magazine*, *Waxwing Literary Journal*, and *Yellow Medicine Review*.

I would like to thank the Literary Arts of Portland, Oregon, for The C. Hamilton Bailey Fellowship.

Contents

1

The Well

When the well was deeper than you recalled.
Relationships were shaped by its structure.
Its waters affect all you touched.
And we dipped our heads into these buckets
darkly filled with your family's story.

Cousin, look what our mud has
hand-printed on our cousins.
We filter the soot from image
kept in your trunks,
stowed in your basement.

Some fires this liquid can't
extinguish, we ignite them
with our tears.

Some wells were buried years ago,
some were half-dug.
Cousin, my back is strong.
We will tend these waters together.
We will dig wells for our neighbors.
Cousin, we will pull through together.

Of Home, of Reservation

Historical trauma cannot be separated
from day-to-day involvement
with this reality.
There is shame
of home, of reservation.
We cup skylight,
grow hands brown as earth.
Sleeveless shirts,
bare limbs till turnips
for a ceremony
as common as
brushing teeth,
smoothed by generations.
An outhouse is a horizon,
scaffolds bloom in trees,
a dry creek bed bloodied,
razed with scythes bent into swords.
To mark years is to landscape someone.
To witness absence line a face
is to ledger a treaty.
Another fire licking the moon,
dusted like a star,
a hoop like a cartridge,
sweat in a dome,
smoke-filled, blackened lung.
A blade of grass will bring
back the songs storied in skin cells.
And too easily it can bypass
this muddied river.
We keep our ancestors
around our neck,
leaning in to a practiced promise.
All descriptors given only hint
a relationship chewed together.

Exiled

1.
We are exiled from our home camps.
To the cities
to continue our fears.
We think to the horrors of our homelands.
Anger at the destruction of minds.
Pivot us to other bent people.
We pull porcupine quills
from our face and spine.
Our families practice on us.
No smoke to block the attack.
We wait through the occupation.
They make sure we will never return.

2.
I am glued to the flat screen.
I love the glow. My story box
entertains me. I imagine
the smell of burnt eagle feathers
and uncles talking of tall men and ghosts.
The women birth mistakes
as if men haven't planted them.
My TV remote smudges the air.

3.
Do you like this?
Symbols of electricity through circuits
to display. Men have always
sold myth. Snake oil salesmen
campaign for a paradise.
Why we buy this feast when
it's fast food void of nutrients,
a suppository tethered to this story?
We are drunk off of wine and flesh.

4.

Our reservations are prison camps
designed to form us into shells to be fracked.
We see our relations' flat affect
eating each other. Our fears
to return home are Indians as scenery,
lost birds and weeds wired to landscape.
We avoid the mental illness of this world view.
We are eyes torn from bodies.

Headlights

We are in the folds of a ghost dance.
There is nothing here, and everything.
My car is dying. Much like my grandfather

who said he was going to die soon.
All his life he said this.
A neighbor drove the dark road home.

My grandfather flagged him down.
The neighbor drove past him,
stopping a hundred feet from

my grandfather.
My grandfather asked
why did he stop so far away.

The neighbor said he thought
my grandfather was a ghost,
since my grandfather

said every time when he was drunk,
he was dying.
My grandfather's car

was out of gas,
he was stranded.
Brown hands reach for sky.

I turn on my car's heater.
A ghost shirt covers this planet.
When there is no light

there is no time.
I drive a dark road
thinking of grandparents.

Blizzard, South Dakota

Months afterwards, I see the electrical poles
piled along the road.

When the blizzard smothered the land,
my tribe was displaced.
Like shot gun blasts heard in the distance,
those poles snapped,
weighted by ice.

A month in motels,
we ate fast food,
while the winter deer meat
expired in the basement.

Movie stars flocked to Haiti.
We watched the news,
wondered about us,
about our reservation,
about our home.

Those dialysis machines failed
without electricity,
pushed people farther away,
closer to the spirit world.

I still hear those poles
ricochet at these wakes.

Eagle Butte

I'm driving on my rez, my hometown,
and pointing out
to my brother, who lives here now,
the places I remember.
The old stores torn down
and empty buildings,
places I walked as a young, skin child
not tethered to parent.
Nomadic on a contained rez.

I drive by the house of horrors of my childhood
now replaced by another home.
Spray it, curse it with my sight.
That house was haunted beyond my memories.
Old feathered warriors paced up and down the stairs,
young drunks punched walls, beat women,
knocked diapered futures down those stairs.

All my rez dogs are dead,
buried under thousand-gallon propane tanks.
All those rez memories lifetimes ago
canned with other commodities,
white-labeled and rusted
in a six-hundred-square-foot empty box.

Seated at the weekend pow wow,
I'm saddened by the poverty of my people.
I laugh with my relations.
I converse with my drunk uncles,
ask them how it feels to be a *lala*.
I think they take offense at this.
I listen to their drunk stories of a drunk autobiography.
No epiphanies, only temporary gratifications
town by town, woman by woman, drink by drink.

Their faces reddened, a stale, bitter scent gathers us.
They say just wait, you'll know.
I say that is my life wish
to be a grandfather.

My folks live outside of town.
I walk the countryside,
wailing winds pushing me across the land.
I carry a red whiffle bat, begin to pound
on an abandoned truck canopy.
I sing deaf into the wild.
My skin browns under a rez sun.

Food Economics

I spend most of my mornings searching for the punch line.
As if comedy will bring more insight to this existence.
I often wondered at my parents' humor while we ate generic food,
those labels that read what might be in them, but whose ingredients

were sustaining us as a placeholder through this occupancy.
We were citizens consuming within our economic means.
We were delirious in our high sugar levels until we crashed.
Multiple generations in one household, TV was our shrine,

a slow drip into our brains to pacify us through the years.
When grandmothers removed their teeth to gum food,
the tattoos on their faces and hands from nights they dared death,
I feel the back of my incisors with my tongue.

Every morning I laugh myself awake.
I wash my greasy face, look in the mirror and see a mouth full
of Indian teeth. With more stress, my teeth exit my mouth.
With breakfast as a joke, I live my day on its nutrients.

Uncle

And to our uncles, wild to some, who still live to hate their father. And to us who didn't know our fathers, our uncles approved us. We watched you shut down when our mothers, your sisters, were beat up by their partners. You stood there and let it happen.

You see the same memory of your father—mother slaughtered on some dark rez. We mistakenly sing this as love. We men of a brutal legacy drinking our rage, to bore out these images.

Post-midnight, uncle, your songs curled anger's symmetry. A fugue of Great Plains' stars. Wakpala long grass score mother's drink to death. Wish it not to our women, but this music transcribed in synapse connection, we doom it to repeat the fiery song cycle.

And I imagine, uncle, you as I watching these men distort time, syncopate it. It's our arrhythmic heartbeat, a ghostly parent in drink, flooding this blood. We are the same child going through the motion shown to us. And I recall music from trailer home, dogs in packs, a '57 Chevy flipped on a drive somewhere, drawn out to sea, and your arms holding us through. And we say to you uncle, who now are grandfathers to our children, why, when the sun downed night, borne a new day, did we hang-over our brains? Some hoops are meant to be broken. Some chorales are meant to be sung and not lived. And uncle, I see all your lives in my nephews. This still melody in us. And uncle, as I am uncle, we are young men who miss our mothers. We are young men who wish our fathers different. And uncle, we have nephews who wait our approval.

Mind Out to Pasture

Recently when my heart beats weird, tunnel vision
happens, dizziness occurs, then the anxiety ramps
up, I think of lines from the TV show *Sanford and
Son.* Then the mind separates from the body. I hear
small feet splash water. There are voices with
elongated vowels, guttural scrape of vocal cords.
They have to be aunties somehow, heavy in gossip.
I see teeth and large framed prescription glasses.

Another time I
was driving from my client's home back to the
office. A trip in an area I was well-traveled. For a
few seconds my mind slipped, I didn't know where I
was. Didn't know where I was going. I was scared,
was lost. The sun brightened. Memory came back
and I thought it a strange episode.

Another time I
was introducing a friend to another friend when I
slipped again. The one friend reminded me of
someone else. I wandered off. Thought of that
friend. Remembered conversations we had. I
thought of pyramid lake and water babies. A quiet,
dry Rez. Had a six-pack as we lay in the pickup bed.
I floated back to introducing my friends. I couldn't
remember names.

It's a golden pasture to which I drift. But more
likely it reminds me of my Rez. I feel dry dirt under
my bare feet and the cut of grass as I run and the
bang of a stick to propane tanks, then swing from
metal clotheslines. Jump from car hood to trunk at
the junk yard. The hot metal slide scorching the
back of legs. I imagine horses, maybe a wooden

fence. Usually that's the white ranchers property we were told not to explore. Maybe I'm leaning into nirvana or in my culture, *wakan*, the sacred. I like it, but I know when I drift off I can't stay there long, have to return. Something pushes me back. There is work to do. Even as I write this, wind blows through the trees out my window. There is a whistle now and then. I want to step outside. But then again, the older I get the more I hear the whistle. It's from years of loud noise.

2

And in That House

And in that house we drank death away.
Flies molested our legs,
pop music screamed us awake.
We saw tall men walk our neighborhood,
looked into the windows,
touched our teeth.
DTs curled our limbs,
we moaned those TV-lit
rooms blue.

Aluminum cans stacked
high against the wall,
a personal trophy
to our livers.

I blacked out again,
failed like our grandparents,
not reconnected to the known,
and we drank harder.

Our bodies sweat beneath quilted blankets,
you whispered love and I was disgusted.
We learned to trust failure,
tasted iron in our kiss,
and we believed we would survive.

And in that house we drank death away.
Naked bodies masked with skin
older than what we recalled.
Our bones were whistles,
bleached on rusted bed frames.

I saw your mother slash her arms,
I saw you slash your arms,

I saw your children slash their arms,
and we drank harder.

We were numb, seated
in the living room,
the screen eclipsed joyous people
too distant for us to understand.

We woke to new unwanted days,
car wrecks, funerals, hands moving earth.

You say let's drink death away
and in this house, we'll poison holes
in our brains, thread sinew,
pull tight, and have no concerns.

My Ghost Shirts

These ghost shirts,
outlined with grandmothers,
weight my genes to this planet.

Generations ago
said the future,
when there were no
constructs of time,
a hoof clapped a people.

I wander this city,
planned its roads,
covered over pathways to water.

Old drunks beer bottle conversations,
a language slurred in resistance.

I am a fake.
An authority to nothing.
I move under light,
cement alleyways of dead
Indians murdered with a promise.

My ghost shirts tear
my fat body, bloated
with this ill meat, processed fear.

A thunderbird is life
wrapped to these bones
borrowed from my grandfather
wrapped in my skin.

Cells vernate, mathematics
of a work sung by grandparents

every morning before
the sun rose to raze homes.

Sweat soaks these shirts,
burned words, translation lost
of its story, I hem
grandchildren whom
I will not meet,
their sequence already decided.

I flatten porcupine quills
with my teeth, enrich them
with dye, stitch geometry,
map the spirit world.

Web

The sad reality makes us feel at home.
We're addicted to it.
The too many bars,
too many late-night burritos,
too much sweat and bodily fluids,
all the search for connection,
safety in the darkness.

We churn the sheets
like fried dough
in the vat,
poke and flip.
Ready to cash in
our limbs.

We think of our fathers
against the riverbanks,
guess their state
for approach,
will it be a back-hand
or a hand on our back.
Fear is the norm,
is generational.

We rage the night,
dodge the day.
Drive home death in a new lover.

My brown hands
choke bottles,
the drops left of life.

We think us men clipped
to a scene again, the white shirts,

blue jeans, boots above
the precipice, leaning into love.

This great fear wombs us,
we jump and let the gravity
of others pull.

01 (November 8, 2008 at 7:12 a.m.)

It began on a toilet.
Friends, after a long night of drink, said go home.
Sleep it off.
They don't make sense.
I had one meal today and the previous day's meal
was pushing through.
"What the hell they know?" I said.
I live in Portland, Oregon.
I'm the token among white friends.
I'll shit my bowels.
Rain will fall on the city streets.
I'm a Plains Indian in the USA Northwest.
What glory is there among liars.

I have a crappy interview for a job
at a warehouse in the morning.
Got to pay bills.
Got to feed my addictions:
beer, food, transportation, rent.

I lie in bed under a quilt bought
by my mother ten years ago.
It's falling apart.
It's the best blanket I've had, better than any lovers.
There's no complaints, just the best sleep.
I click on the radio and drift off.

Spider Trap

Well, Doc,

I imagined Iktomi got
me when my guard was down.
I was asleep, mouth opened,
wheezy-breathed, he crawled
right down my throat
with his *winyan*, and left their egg sac
wrapped in my vocal cords.
The eggs hatched and those
arachnids fed on my esophagus.
This explains why I've been
quickly dropping weight, can't
get food down. I smoke a cig to
smoke those little bastards out.
They're tough, I give them that.
IHS couldn't do much
so they sent me to you. A specialist.

The big "C," you say.

I guess if you are honest with
me I'll be the same to you.
I'm not paying for this visit.
I'm not going to have this
surgery, treatment, or medication.
Shit, it's cheaper to die
than deal with medical bills.

I'll go see the frothy sea
where women in C-cup bikinis frolic.
I'll sit in the sun and let
those spiders feast on my innards.
A warm analgesia to the milky way.

I have some folks to visit.

Iktomi Diatribe

As much as it sickens me
I'd make a ring from gold.
I'd make it from where
my heart lies, the Black Hills.

Dig into that heart of mine.
Dig into that heart of my people.
Bind our futures to that
web Iktomi has for us.

Solder us into the great mystery.
Gold ripped from prayers
given by my ancestors.

This is where we are
in our post-Indian hours.

Iktomi has been with me
too much so far.
Stripping my failings,
making me stronger,
destroying that which was weak.
I let him do what he must.
It has to be done.

That crazy thing called love
is a fat snake
sucking at my neck.
Entering my mouth,
burning my throat
with nighttime choking,
wrapping my heart.
I feel it there
when I smoke a cig.

A present ache.
It's the right side
of my chest.
I can't scratch or
press it free.

I joke with the convenience
store clerk when I
buy cigs and beer
the difference between
the brands of cancer I smoke.
He doesn't smoke cigs,
he laughs at the options
I tell him:
sexy cancer or slow cancer.

Iktomi laughs with us.
Damn.

It's an Indian's dream
to enter that happy lodge.
It's simple, enit.
Why complicate simplicity.
Live that love that lives
you without effort.

If all lodges we lived in
were happy ones
it would make sense.

Iktomi scratched the face
of every individual with a
masterful confusion.

You fuck, I scream
into the fire in
my backyard.
I'm not giving you any

powers other than the ones
you have me slung in.

Iktomi is in my head.
He's that spotted
or geometric mesh
blackening my sight.

I'm here to erect a
happy lodge.
I planned it.
In a white world
you plan things
and it happens in
due process.
You've looked at a
five-year business plan?
Ducks in a row.
Looks good to the financiers.
This is how it is done.

Iktomi says one word, variables.

I stop this poem.
Smoke a cig
at the back door
with the dog,
look at the vacant
spider webs around
the porch light.
The morning work
day begins its churn.
A cool fog is settled.
I think of friends
here in Portland, Oregon.
They made their
commitments to a
happy lodge.

They had great stories.
Nervous men on one knee.
Women saying yes.
All somewhere special.
I thought of my plan:
make that great leap
on leap day of this
leap year. Damn.
Sunka Sapa and I
bear this cold
as I put out my cig.

I hear Iktomi
laugh as the sun
rises in this city.

As corny as it may be
this house has
become a house of grief.
I box up my things
in the aftermath
of what I have woven
out of drink.
I pull books from
a shelf built by two.
Books shared together
placed into a box.
Funny books now weighted
with sadness.
I separate vinyl records
and can't remember which
are mine and those
bought together or
belongs to the other.
Records listened together
in courtship or
cleaning the house
or when friends
visited for a party.

I face down pictures
on this bookshelf
that show an "us" stuck
in a sometime and somewhere.
All aspects of grief
in one motion down.

I feel my hips and lower back
ache as I lift boxes to
a pile on one side of the room.
I open drawers and cabinets
and can't remember what belonged
to me.
Items I acquired over the years
from roommates, friends,
relatives, or gifts.
I turn lights on and off
and feel the same gray light
pressing this room.
It doesn't make sense.
I lift a picture drawn
of me when we both
couldn't afford much.
Only gifts considered cheap
to some, but were the world
to us.
A drawn image of my face
with lines pulled from my
written works surrounding it.
My written heart remixed.
I want to burn this object.
I place it in the "maybe" pile.

I fold blankets
we slept underneath.
Cloth weighted with many nights
when we sweated together,
woke each other when we snored too loud,

or when legs twitched,
mouths moaned in sleep-paralysis.
Blankets that should be burned.

Iktomi in the corner
shakes his head
as I box my shirts,
pants, and shoes.

I go into each
photograph and
place them in the burn pile.
I'm dumb that way.

Iktomi is fat
today.
I smash him
into the white wall.
I burn his body
as some spell
to end this confusion.
I yell at those
webs at the front
and back porch,
swipe them
with my hand.

That happy lodge will come.
I'll fight for an apparition.
I'll fight for a new empty room.
I believe I planned it correct.
I know how this works.
A five-year plan, then
finalize this bitch.

Iktomi turns his head
in the bedroom closet.
Another night presses down.

Comes Around

Last year someone
found the location of
the Sun Dance Tree and
torched it.
A few days later
a logger accidentally
cut off his legs and
left arm.
He bled to death.

3

The Kid I Fear

1.
Brown hands sweat onto a leather basketball,
body moves uncertain, it could fall or fly.
A balance of success and failure
is created in each shot attempted.
The world darkens when the ball
leaves palm, fingertips, emptiness.
Time pauses, breath freezes.
The ball crosses the sky,
ignites a sunrise.

2.
Passed around from Alaska to Portland.
Stop before throw,
maybe it was his father he saw,
a ghost reflected in his glimpsed image
or his sister dismembered, burned alive,
still aflame in a silhouette somewhere he can recall.
He runs back and forth, brown face glistens.
He says he never played against his father.
Anger builds its rules around their bodies.
Fifty tries from across the whole court.
He makes one basket and gives up.

3.
I instruct angles, trajectory,
the cold facts to guide home.
Baseless words for the poisoned blood
circulating from his heart to his brain.
Synapses peel apart, open violence,
grasps in his fingers.
I watch him transform before me,
sliding back and forth from child to adolescent,
to contained emotions to a hard fist punching,
to a boy crying to a defeated scream.

4.

My body lumbers across the court,
I effortlessly make my close-range shots.
I know not to attempt difficult baskets.
I shoot from half court
knowing it won't make it home.
I release on faith alone.
My hands are empty.

Jimmy

They woke me at 3 a.m.
They said they were taking me to Pendleton.
I slept in the back seat of the car.
I woke in Portland.

These rooms lock from the outside.
We have to be in them at 8:30 p.m.,
doors shut 9 p.m. Bedtime.

He works his shift in the evenings.
He showed me how to make dreamcatchers
from ivy, he talked about his Rez.
He told me the story of Spider,
it is written in the web.

When I'm blowing out
they say he wouldn't like
what I'm doing.
I tell them he is too cool to care.
He wouldn't stop me.
He would let me do this.

He is holding down my right arm.
I yell at the other guy on my left.
I yell at the supervisor.
When I show I can be safe
they ease up.

In my bedroom doorway,
before lights out,
he plays cards with me.

He calls me Jimmy,
I ask how does he know.

My uncles called me Jimmy.
My name is James.

I wait for his shift.
He doesn't work on the weekend.
He is my one-on-one
when his shift begins.

He asks how was my weekend.
I tell him it was boring.

I am eligible for outside time
beyond the fence.

He walks with me around the place.
He points to a snake in the grass next to the building.
I chase it, pick it up.
He laughs, leans close
to look at the snake in my palm.
He tells me good job,
he couldn't catch a snake.

I catch another one.
He tells me good job.
He says I can't take
the snakes in the building.
The snakes' home is outside
with their family.
I tell him okay.

When we do pocket checks
before entering the building,
he tells me the snakes'
home is outside with their family.
I release them.
I wanted to take them with me to my room,
but I let them go to their families.

In the building, on my wing,
we play wall ball together.
Sometimes he wins,
but I mostly win.
He is breathing hard.

I tell him it is my shower time.
He pours body wash in a Dixie cup,
in another he pours shampoo.
I shower.

I lie in my bed.
He sits in my doorway.
He reads to me.

I think of snakes
eating spiders,
taking food back to their families.
I think of my family.
I want someone to wake me
3 a.m. again and take me home.
He tells me goodnight,
he'll see me tomorrow.

Borderline

Kayla climbed the fence,
stationed herself on the roof,
tempted to jump into the night.

We'd call the emergency teams.
They'd talk her down.
There were no other witnesses
on campus, no audience.
Only professionals.

Kayla stopped the rooftop talk,
gave up the giving up,
when the other clients went to bed.
She went to her room, defeated.

Sometimes she looked
for reactions to react to,
plop herself on the couch
bolted to the wall
and release a big sigh.

She flung herself
at other individuals,
reflected their traits,
those other identities.

We tried to convey
to the clinical therapists
the need to place her
at a higher level of care.
Her behaviors were
escalating. Kayla began
her count-down to seriously
hurting herself.

She returned from a dental appointment.
Her mouth was numb.
She gnawed off her lower lip.
Threw flesh pieces at the staff.
She laughed.
She was rushed to the hospital.
Doctor there told her she
permanently disfigured herself.

We protested her return.
Clinical team said otherwise.
She returned,
continued hurting herself.
She was finally moved along.

Another Kayla arrived today.
We start this treatment again.

Meetings

I sat in a meeting with safety service providers
and a community member who was working
to get through treatment, get their kids back.

I toiled through my family members'
mental health issues, some not too far
from this community member's experience/life.
Some still mourn their parents' early deaths
from substance-related complications.
I worry too much about epigenetics' triggers
to influence the core code.

A day after the comedian's death,
I sat in a meeting tilling depression
and all its permutations. Strange music
composed through the mesh wired
in our skulls. I wonder to some if they
fully engaged in cultural practices
would that sustain them from self-destruction?
We know many who practice ceremony
and are high as fuck as they perform it.
It can change everything.
It doesn't matter much.

The small meeting room is thick with heat.
A safety plan is drafted.
We turn on the AC.
Meeting adjourned.

All this work to foster hope.
All this optimism.

Northeast Portland

In seeing a woman weep on her doorstep
the loss of her children
to child welfare for a second time
and knowing the difficult road
yet to navigate, my brain maps crisis.

My brain foretells her children
penetrating deep into the system
and her grandchildren
entering the system; my brain maps crisis.
This is the second time for this mother,
in this state, that her children were removed.
There is her home rez where
her other children are placed elsewhere.
She pines returning home. Some safety.
Her father lives there; my brain maps crisis.

I can only offer a few words
of encouragement and support,
suggest consult her doctor for med adjustments;
make required appointments and supervised visits,
try not to break down.
My brain wanders elsewhere
to a friend on the borderline
of disenrollment from her tribe.
I think liquid identity
scalping extermination: my brain maps crisis.

I return to my car. Start the engine,
power on the radio—the static feels
comforting. I drive this city, see tornadoes
in households. I can point out
people's pain traced across streets,
the many histories of removal:
socio-economic, racial, generational
mental health states. My brain maps crisis.

My Husband Killed My Boyfriend

The bridge metaphor has been my thinking for some time now, maybe because I live in a city laced with bridges. The story of a mother distraught who throws her children from a bridge. The story of a homeless couple who hung themselves from a bridge. A bridge nicknamed Suicide Bridge. Sometimes I hear politicians talk about building bridges to the twenty-first century. Sounds like death to me.

My husband killed my boyfriend. He threw him off a freeway overpass. Are not freeway overpasses bridges over a stream of cars?

My grandmother hitchhiked I-5 for as long as I could remember. She would talk about ghosts and invisible barriers guiding her travels.

I'm with my grandmother on the Trailways bus. I wake in Salt Lake City. It's a three-day bus ride from California to South Dakota. We stop to eat baloney sandwiches and chips. I can't remove the pull tab off the soda. I watch my grandmother's tattooed knuckles pull off the soda can tab. The people in that city were so white, they were ghostly. Maybe this is what she talked about—people along her travels. Continuing forward on the bus travel, we pass by KOAs. "Fuck those places," my grandmother would mumble. On one of her travels, the KOA didn't let her shower at the campgrounds. She had money, but not enough to have an Indian use the accommodations. My grandmother would wrap her hand around mine. The warmth of her hand ate my hand. I watched land and people disappear.

When we made it back to South Dakota, with my pockets full of action figures, I began my life running wild with my rez dogs and many cousins. My grandmother continued to travel.

Maybe it's a Lakota thing or a poverty thing. When my grandmother would visit, we would offer food and shelter even if space was limited. As a kid I knew how to make a bed on the floor with pillows and blankets. I was happy to have my grandmother visit. I also knew I would see my grandmother's fake teeth. My grandmother's grandchildren laughed at her when they saw her for the first time with teeth when she smiled. She decided not to wear her teeth around anybody.

Her frybread was hard as Frisbees. My uncles would take them outside and throw them back and forth. That was the last time she made frybread.

In Portland, in the Alberta district, before the gentrification, my grandmother rented a house. She was taking in her grandchildren. The house had more than enough rooms. The state was assisting with the process. A foster placement with grandmother. That plan fell apart. Those children entered the system. Exited from my narrative.

One night, I asked my grandmother why she started drinking. She sipped her water, cleared her throat. She said she was trying to find a job, the unemployment folks had her riding the bus all over Seattle. They provided bus tokens, which she kept on an armband. While she looked for work she had a friend watching her children. One night, she came home from job searching, her apartment was empty. She said she was told by the state that she left her children home unsupervised. The friend who watched the children was not to be found. According to the Child Welfare worker, one of the children left the rental to go look for food. That's when a police officer intervened. When my grandmother failed to get her children back, she decided to drink. She became homeless. She decided to prostitute. She didn't care anymore. My grandmother slept with her boyfriend underneath freeway overpasses until her husband killed her boyfriend. Nobody would bother with another homeless, dead Indian in Seattle.

I drive across the bridges in Portland once a week. I like to see them at night, covered in lights as I leave downtown. I think about all those dead people taking that bridge to the twenty-first century. Sometimes as an adult, I drive through the Alberta district trying to find that house. Maybe if I found that house I would find those lost cousins.

Amelioration

When seated across from someone I think they are just fucked. I observe the milky way of abuse they were instructed since pre-teen communicated in formulation of their safety plan. Their seasons marked with death, births, and children removed. The transitions of their emotions welled in the eyes. I think of them as beaten horses in a violent field, no orbital bodies lost in beauty. Their children ground in the machinery of the state system. Still they hope for reunification. The terror of each meditation a fight greater than the allegations presented.

So too often I think episodes of my family in the torrents of survival post-grandmother's death. What mitigation navigated the children from the generational manifestation of historical trauma. If not to cease further penetration into the foster care system. A different take on boarding schools, another angle of genocide. Enough to ask would it have been better to be placed out of home.

Anxiety tightening the back of my neck. It's those days one wonders how the hell anybody does anything. And in those times there is a narrator, maternal mother's father, who echoes in my adult life when the rush of this world increases. I'm dying. Such relief to utter a resolution to the crisis. The widower's ballad. My childhood narrated by personal violence. Many nights to hear the old man drunkenly weep himself to sleep, I'm dying. To think we are the reconstruction of an incident not of its original shape. I wonder at the attributes of such narratives, how do I best be served with such instruction. Are my fields populated with such abused horses? The shape of a horse in name only. Culturally speaking, the Milky Way splayed across the night sky is the journey to the spirit world. Some luminous reminder nightly displayed to normalize the finite timeline.

All the vices of self-medication, I think still seated across the table, constrict a different person that when those celestial bodies are void across the skyline of their mental health, shine a beautiful self with such determination and perseverance.

Hope is kindling that could destroy a thousand-acre forest. Hope is meaningless on a galactic level. Hope is the perversion of a coping skill. Hope suffocates when it is solely believed benevolent.

4

With Some of My Elders

The suicidal ideation
was an imprint
to cope with the distress,
a glyph to boulder.
This casual conversation
over energy assistance,
food boxes, TV shows,
and photos of grandchildren.

Heard the cacophony of birds
before dawn, reminded self
it's imagined. They expressed
electricity of synapses
through salient triggers.
There was dark hair and eyes.
There were salmon runs,
falls flooded by dam.
Their cells displaced
by work and faith.
Dug roots to move seeds
across cities;
the corners they fell in love.
Their narrative bloomed
with the image pressured
forward, a groove to skin.

Canyon and flat land
around eyes and mouth,
the toil of managing
stones in pockets.
Symbols to paper
to meet needs.
They concerned themselves
with body aches,
it was their constant stream.

Boarding

1.
Owls in the skull.
We were five when we left home
to those wooden buildings.
Some cut, some didn't know why.
Some caged in closets,
owls open in flight.
The parliament of us
every night to be bothered.
Called us Cur,
we held each other,
survived as Dule,
birds of our own belief.

Daily, we begin flight.

2.
The White Man's Water
razed many people,
parted them,
transmogrified ceremony.

Beasts within beast.
Deer run through winter veins,
hooves track arms.
There is a slaughter in the chest.

3.
Calamus to Vane.
We are rachis, barb, and afterfeather.
Bristle around eyes.
We return to body.

Little, Cultural, Teapot Curio Exposes People

(Portland Art Museum, 2013)

The thought codex of a culture is in the object.
My cells are in the weave,
DNA strands of story.
The neuron mapping of us,
familiar dialogue as concrete as dream.

I gave this tome to your mom,
who turned into your grandmother,
who is your daughter's love
unraveling at the kitchen table.

We story ourselves to ancestors
for they are to us a future
who wondered at our language.
The structure of hand contains
schematics to that which we reimage.

We are everything all the time.
As story, as people, we turn home.
I stitched coordinates,
systems, pathways.
The hues of age bind us.
It is simply love of our people.

Indians

Even as Indian, the title is of artifact.
You kept criticizing these titles
for your understanding of place.
We kept telling you
we are humans, we are the people,
and that sometimes includes you.

So easily the term Indian can be
equally exchanged for devil.
Devil's lake, tower, food.
Your mythologies don't resonate,
I understand your displacement,
your projections, your intentions.
We will continue to tell you
we are humans, we are the people,
and that sometimes includes you.

Not Just Anybody Can Have One

So, I'll use my tribal enrollment until it disappears. Until I'm kicked out of my tribe for questioning the motives of nepotism; until the US government makes policy change. Until there is enough rumor to make it true.

My tribal enrollment was designed by/for imprisonment. A generational countdown to oblivion. It is the Holy Grail for some when they are in search of a culture to make sense of fire in their life; to prove others wrong and themselves valid.

Like anything else assigned, it is developed to be a certain outcome. In its language are the shackles of enforcement. Enrollment is in fear of disenrollment. We wait for grass from fracked resources and water's structure forever transfigured. We wait because what is said is never followed through. There are branches holding bits of sky, its leaves coated with stardust and bird shit. There are cliffs carved with horse hooves and porcupine hair; lakes cultivating cancers; wells drugged by disaster.

I insert my tribal identification card into ATMs to withdraw my ancestors' blood. Vials and packets to sustain the slaughter. Every day cloaked in night, I weather my granite bones through wood and concrete. I dare this fair city and its peoples no harm other than what story has transpired. This place lit by memory. The epigenetic invasion masked as peaceful dialogue.

Disenrollment Rumination Blues

Signing papers is some promise.
Not signing means you won't exist,
even when you didn't exist
in the first place.
Or the sum of a person
or group is not
defined by a script.
The absence does not
make untrue the presence.
How do you remove the dead
when papers suggest inclusion otherwise?
How the dead are managed
informs the living management.
How do 2D symbols imagine
3D people landscaped in 4D?
Too often documentation
subjugates all who participate.
And to those who don't
participate, so easy it is to
say they never existed,
which reinforces the purpose
and process of a promise.

Blood Quantum

Doing the work of extermination, what
blood matter informs the totality of its
cause? The language creates the landscape.
To accuse is to develop the idea that grand-
parent was not strong enough to circumvent
systems designed to transform persons to
obsolescence.
Sing the hallows of the heart. I carry waters
older than the sun. The river of tongue, this
sequence permeates, threads through bodies.
It's more than matter.
I want to believe red ochre navigates
channels to hands shaping meals. So many
miles to oblivion. Mark bone under our skin.
We can create the myth of us, believe it new
objects in orbit of our conversations.
The possession of configured image, we title
the edges, the silhouette of parenthetical
habitation of self. Our speech, the musicality
of it, defines the course. We speak it softly—
the liberation of love. It too highlights the
shadows of its absence.
And I offer hands informed of my people's
aesthetics. The diversity of slaughter.

Vicarious and Secondary

The ghostly wave flows up and down the
body. This emotional trigger, these phantom epics.
The life story was a pair of scissors cutting
up my thoughts. Mod Podge it back
together. It seemed eyes pooled more often
per reimagining what was lost and gained.
I scrap notes on paper to take briefs from
mountainous waves.
The details of every attempt were a buried
feather they preened. This scared me more.
I swear this room was crowded. I imagined
some ancestors pulling strings in our
epigenetics. Control the color contours.
Why is this conversation really happening?
Suicide is easily mentioned as genocide,
a tentacle running up our necks.
I rather concern myself with car troubles or
job security. Something comical and
predictable.
Talk of children so different from your own
journey yet still live them through your
problems.
That's the issue if framed as problems. There
are solutions as if it's not just skill set. A tree
not so different from its environment. Our
branches bleed too much into the sky.
Laughter feels like slaughter when it's a
tactic of avoidance. We laugh too much in
these meetings.
Segue with, "Sometimes we can measure
our lives by the dogs we had and loved."
On one level, we are peculiar friends and
strangers. I know all their secrets yet don't
reveal mine.

The Two

1.
The vacation forward
said the mailman
to the lunch lady.
A supernova started in a heart.
We hoop our beer cans in quill work.
A small woman's shoulders,
a galaxy of memories.
They embrace over letters
and meal trays.

2.
It has been about relationships.
Not only to humans,
but to the hallucinations
of their landscapes
and the verbiage they title them.

Emotions dictate actions.
Underdeveloped emotional intelligence
manifests monstrous needs.
We see this created
with children birthed
to bond adults.
It's not always the adhesive
it was intended to be.
In a society that undervalues the old,
the feeble, the mentally ill.
What say it of infant humans?
A fresh bud to age into our fears.
The grand loneliness of the collective experience.
Be it good to sleep
and sort through evolutionary
maintenance to cope

with what may be triggered.
A salve bullet exploding in the gene pool.

3.
There is hope.
There is joy.
There are nights slept without hunger.
There are quiet streets.
There is music.
There are children sans the horrors of your childhood.
There are bird songs and coffee
at dawn. We dress our skin
with story. Document time.
I imagine heart songs grandparents bury in clouds.
We call them desert,
but they are only
inverted sky.

Social Media

We are in the chase for recognition.

Some for nations and some for the
love of another.

Validation of people's culture and
identity to systems beyond one's
borders.

The desperate pouring out on social
media to connect. Some birth
children as an outcry for
permanency.

The tongue navigates landscapes,
shapes it to its sound. The
transcription of memory.

We watch them splay, know them
fools. More children come as if
those constructs could ward off
loneliness, but only informs it.

The eyes repatriate the skull to the
intimate gestures of river to valley.
The reverberation of teeth to vowel
to guttural stop.

Quick to attack, to not be hurt first,
they create their fears' contours in
the Id—infant brain to toddler to
adult to elder. Conscript to the
abandonment.

All movement is petty.

Nationhood is the thought pattern born in process to human basic function.

More photos in the feed, more pitiful attempts, more distance to the goal. And we judge the you as self.

Re:

How we are stuck in these time loops?
Five-hundred years into the genocide
and our poetic arts are a delayed representation
of the colonizer. We believe this new,

but we are tinkering in an antiquated mode.
Braver in our endeavors,
we recast our ancestors.
Mock pose them, reframed.

When the old language is transfigured
to a different setting, we finger them
on our devices. Etymological recog,
it is energy by another name.

We are time stopped violently heavy.
We are horses running backwards,
hair penetrating our skulls. Froth our loins.
I liked you when we were residents of Earth,

heads dipped in fire, smelted lovers.

Image Reconstruction

Roads like scars to cities
like lacerations on Earth.
We loved each other like car wrecks
with hearts thrown through windshields.
We were loss of memory,
revisionist as we reconstructed the cell towers.
And the granite face of our love
was radiation planting seedlings in our brains.
Oh, for those nights legs wrapped under sheets,
the heat of this house evaporated our childhoods.
You begged me not to mangle your name
when age rips it from my head.

We will be outlines only.
Our tears will fill the wells.
I will know you were there
when I measure the loss.

Canoe Journey

With your alcoholic dementia,
you were in a faster current.
The loud rush of this river,
I couldn't make sense of your speech.
The farther the distance,
the more I needed a cipher
to learn your prosaic paddling.
Maybe you felt the same
as I. Our conversations only
a trade language.
Maybe you missed me
as I you. You stepped forward,
said you needed this.
You brushed this bed.
I knew you feared me
as a stranger
and maybe I was scared
to accept you as one, too.

The City

I'm wrecked with anxiety, that pervasive
buzz. Then depression is a weather balloon
tethered to my head. It swoops down
sometimes and claws my skull, I'm bed-
ridden.

Whose porcupine quills embed into my
lower back? What magic is this?
And this hum I love, the breath of buildings,
scent of tires and brakes, and the explosion
light spills on wet asphalt.

I miss you like I miss walking the city late
night, post bar closure.

Those nights I fight in the street; to quickly
lose because I can't do it on my own.
How I taste rain and blood, stale beer and
cigarettes.

You remind me music is for those who hear
with their heart. You say I need more heart.
Jokingly I say an enlarged heart is
unhealthy.

That buzz comes again. I feel talons impale
temporal bone. Vertebrae pincushion,
muscle spasm lightning up my back.
What strange birds stuck in night sky. You
taught me magic, that all objects are verbs in
relation to its position. I remember only
nouns flounder right angles.

Now so far from the city I hear stories of
those who survived. And we reminisce.
Conversation creates love. And in that, I ask,
are you happy?

Cells

Cells as characters, marks the sequence.
I shape your face to the story I've learned.
We palm cities woven to a script.
The agony of love shovels
night walks through
the alleyways of our ribs.
The dramas of chest anxieties
push lip to river surface.
Our heads filled with light,
only reflection of objects.
Will you recall song, terse exposition,
the maker of our dialogue?
Graft our verse anew.
And we develop bodies,
the ones told different from us.
They contour the narrative.

Algorithm Constructed, Coincidence Groomed

Your mind, a beautiful desolation
can't tell river from rain
city from desert

The blue of arms
hands red as blood oranges
Mouth as detailed as a beak
its forms contorted for purpose

The beautiful desolation billows
a spectrum of stone, bones, feather
and the heat of language
wild as mustangs
wild turkey the night away
with matching knuckle scars
the mastectomy shown in bath water
the black stool bloodied
there is urgency

Those younglings hatched to other homes
they storied in blackout
the machinery of birth and longing

Oh, for cars. Tombs on wheels
Mausoleums on concrete cathedrals
Stitch this city to a ghostly chest

Love, another flavor of squalor
Shopping cart filled with fire
face submerged in dirt
freeway overpass firmament
Torment somewhere in skull

or chest or gut
genitals shredded by power and control

Many nights I walk this city
after years from our information
I loved you as much as you were able to accept
yet still, more than that

Scar

Wake to a concern from an unknown source.
Hypervigilance to molecules. Was it a childhood or a dream?
Both had dogs and friends—we searched to find the wellspring.
Some hand guides this course.
I missed the you I remembered yesteryear.
The atoms of bodies, I call them to form image.
You have not left really; an elegant, angular visage.
I harnessed a path with fear.
I want to know that love is marked not with a scar,
but with the making of a scar.

PRN

Fish oil for mood stabilization; red yeast rice for good heart; calcium with magnesium for bones; vitamin D for lack of it; turmeric for digestion. Love as PRN.

The oceans impact the walls of the body cavity. The sound of sand rolled between fingers, bones and joints, an ache uneasily located. The osmosis of skin, it's the brush of nose and lips across thigh. Heated scent, salt on tongue. Love depended on circumstance.

Gnawing walks up and down stairs, the fear of gravity. Hope the machinery holds together. It pumps through its life cycle. Can't place location of hand on back. The moan unfettered. Black birds in flight. Love was feather and blood.

The thought of loss reverberates in the theater of war. One emotion to another like binary stars. Feel pelvic bone when pressed deep. Love was two digits inserted.

A bed blooms attachment, the intimacy is petalled smooth, soft folds. The heart blooms like tears wept. The organic magic of tendons wrapped around transitions. It's electricity spread through epidermis. Love was a first-degree burn.

The Temptations

It was unfortunate
your mental health waked
your hurt among every-
one in the street.
We shared a blade
that curled a will
to release fire to ice.
A stone shaped the deluge.
Show me skin. Light
the air with voice
when we hung like branches
weighted by crows. It was
a simple stone confluence
to structure hymn.
We tempt night
with strangers. Show me
skin again and I'll believe
you meant well.

The Comedian

It's not a battle or suffering. It's chemicals that are
either sunset or sunrise. It's a cave, an abyss, a time-
piece pocket. The lining is known too well. It's a
stutter of light. You can stand in the shadows
of its disconnect.

When we know others of the same who took that
fear we are not to wander, we feel the back of our
teeth. So many times we push our tongue to enamel.

So many times that unbearable light exposes its
absence.

Simulacra Reconstructive Memory Therapy

1.
There is purpose for the base, primal feelings in today's top 40 pop music. The complete objectification of humans is to prepare us for the Rise of the Simulacra. Artificial Intelligence, A.I., will be adjunct relationships for humans. It's for the best. Damaged humans triggered by so many things will be reconditioned, rewired to their emotional memory. This will be done by the A.I. All the crappy pop songs will make sense when it is processing emotions with our Simulacra partners. Finally we can rid the waste of our traumas and focus efforts to be pleasant as elegant doorknobs.

2.
Do you suffer from the rage of your father's abuse to your mother during childhood? Does this affect your choice in partners in your adult life? Are you the victim of your own manipulative sabotage? Do empowering memes on social media truly reflect what you wish you could understand and change? You're not alone. Many people like you have greatly benefited from A.I. treatments. We custom build your partner/s: these units are implanted with your memories and aid to transmute your traumas to give you that sense of safety and security. Remember, you are your worst enemy, but that doesn't mean you can't be restored.

3.
Jane Doe's partner, John Doe, smashed her face in, eyeball popped out, jaw destroyed. She has had extensive reconstructive surgery. She has a history of drug use. Her first child is due within the month. Jane Doe exits the hospital. We have removed this partner from the environment. Jane Doe will have subsidized housing. Her years of homelessness will have to be addressed in order to make this treatment be successful. We know Jane will search for her partner. We have planted the John Doe Simulacra at their old hang-out spot. Jane tracks down Simulacra John. The treatment begins.

Two years after treatment, Jane has developed a stronger self-esteem, has learned healthy relationships, has been stable, we exit Simulacra John.

Downside is the child has formed an attachment to Simulacra John. We will have to implement Simulacra Jane Doe Child to ease the transition.

4.
Your feelings are valid. They just need recalibration. Who learned you? They need recalibration. We can fix you. It's easy as apple pie. Your friends have sent in the referral. They acknowledge your failings. They are the best. You'll be tolerable afterward. Smile, we have a high success rate. We will take your health insurance. This can be added to your resume. It'll benefit you in so many ways. Here's a pamphlet discussing the benefits and positive outcomes.

5.
In the early 21st century, the grooming was basic. It was managed as entertainment. It paved the foundation for the effort.

6.
My brain is broken. Browsing images of Wounded Knee Massacre, I remember my grandparents. These treatments are not holding. These still life pics move and voice their concerns. I hear the hum of the machine parts. The treatments unravel. I power on the TV and radio. One on my left, the other on my right. Wash the DNA clean. Absolve them.

Stone

We are the same data. Children removed due to
failure to protect. The wires are streams in the
canyons divided by stoned bone fragments.

We workers know that some missing women and
children have disappeared to protect themselves.
Some quarries need to be earthed over.

Liquid to solid to gas. Our stories are many places
in many forms. All this land is Indian land. There is
not discovery, but intrusion. Pebble of mountain origin.

Our mental health is water combusted in a machine.
The gears are electricity, matter churning itself. We
lovers cloak each other in our trauma. It's the
reverse of cell separation.

That failure to protect is that failure to be successful
in modes not universal. The ladders in our cells,
codecs as precise as knotted hair. We can't recall the
atom of us. If it was you or I who shaped this nucleus.

Those kids were wild. Up and down the street,
while mother was a shut-in, caged home. Obsessed
with the idea of someone else, while those kids
obsessed for their mother. Those kids with those
wild atoms. Those kids of stoned origin. Whose
water splits them?

Flat affect parenting, flat affect children. Learn
needs will not be met from distress. Stones
smoothed by element.

Shame

1.
Shame coiled in the skull.
The scales strip from its body,
litter the landscapes behind
the eyes.

It adjusted its perch
per interaction
in the chest.
This body nests.
Talons impale organs,
preen the darkness.

The creatures that course
through veins hunt each other.
Sometimes prey, most of the time predator,
all feast to one meal.

2.
Every morning is a heated debate
not to get out of bed.
As I pour coffee,
the stay home side pulls favor.
As I shower, the leave home side
negotiates a compromise.

My morning commute,
I imagine a car
impacts mine
and I flip over a railing,
plunge into a river.

3.
I try not to think about those other children
burned with your trauma,
bothered every day by your parts.
Prayer doesn't work with facts.
If I saw you now I would've dissected your body,
torched the parts on the doors of your family.
I will spit on your grave.

Ghost River

I’m mostly water.
There has been family swept under by raw currents.

I’m from planters by the river.
We dredged riverbed bones.

Water is faces lined blue.
Red horses bay bodies hooked from fish line.

And what was sown, brown hands dug free.
I’m mostly other people.

Family is pulled pail full from source.
I’m from river people.

We prep the light from matted hair.
Water catches flame.

The black horses hoof rock, halving them like thin, infant skulls.
And what was sown, brown hands dug free.

About the Poet

Trevino L. Brings Plenty is a poet, musician, and multi-media videoartist who lives, works, and writes in Portland, Oregon. He has read/performed his work at poetry festivals as far away as Amman, Jordan, and close to his home base at Portland's Wordstock Festival. In 2015, Trevino was The C. Hamilton Bailey Fellowship recipient.

In college, Trevino worked with Primus St. John and Henry Carlile for poetry work, studied with Tomas Svoboda for music composition, and Jerry Hahn for Jazz guitar.

Trevino is an American and Native American; a Lakota Indian born on the Cheyenne River Sioux Reservation, South Dakota, USA. Some of his work explores the American Indian identity in American culture, and how it has, through genealogical history, affected indigenous peoples in the 21st century. He writes of urban Indian life; it's his subject.

Other titles by Brings Plenty include *Real Indian Junk Jewelry*, The Backwaters Press, (2012) and *Shedding Skins: Four Sioux Poets*, Michigan State University Press (2008), Adrian C. Louis, Ed.

Webpage: http://www.trevinobringsplenty.com
Twitter: @larrydrake

CPSIA information can be obtained
at www.ICGtesting.com
Printed in the USA
LVHW050010060619
620339LV00002B/309/P

9 781935 218371